TAFSIR OF SHORT SURAHS FOR MUSLIM YOUTH

BY SHAYKH AḤMAD AL-MAZROOÏ

ISBN: 978-1-7923-8582-7

First Edition: Rajab 1443 A.H. / February 2022 C.E.

Cover Design: Aljadeed Design Co.
Website: www.Aljadeed.Design

Translator: Rasheed Barbee

Editing & Interior Book Design: Razan Gregory

Publisher's Information:
Authentic Statements Publishing
P. O. Box 15536
Philadelphia, PA. 19131
215.382.3382
215.382.3782-Fax

Store:
5000 Locust Street (Side Entrance)
Philadelphia, Pa 19139

Website: www.authenticstatements.com
E-mail: info@authenticstatements.com

Table of Contents

Introduction

بِسْمِ اللَّهِ الرَّحْمَٰنِ الرَّحِيمِ

All praises belong to Allāh, the One who sent down the Qur'ān without difficulty, and may Allāh exalt the rank and send peace upon the one whom Allāh sent to explain the Qur'ān. O Allāh, exalt the rank and send peace upon Prophet Muḥammad and upon his companions, and those who follow them in goodness, those who recite the Qur'ān and listen to it, those who teach it, and those who learn it.

As to what follows:

This concise explanation was written for the Muslim children and youth,[1] and includes Sūrah al-Fātiḥah and some short chapters beginning with Sūrah Aḍ-Ḍuḥā and ending with Sūrah an-Nās. This was written to allow them to understand the general meaning of the Qur'ān so they can ponder over it, benefit from it, and work according to it.

Allāh ﷻ said:

﴿ كِتَابٌ أَنزَلْنَاهُ إِلَيْكَ مُبَارَكٌ لِّيَدَّبَّرُوا آيَاتِهِ وَلِيَتَذَكَّرَ أُولُو الْأَلْبَابِ ﴾

(This is) a Book (the Qur'ān) which We have sent down to you, full of blessings, that they may ponder over its Verses, and that men of understanding may remember.

(Sūrah Ṣād: 38:29)

[1] This explanation is taken from the *tafsīr* of Ibn Kathīr, Sa'dī, Baghawī, and others.

The wisdom for Allāh ﷻ sending down the Qur'ān is so the people can reflect over its verses, extract the knowledge from it, and ponder over its subtleties and wisdom. By pondering the Qur'ān, reflecting over its meanings, and reviewing it over and over, the person will attain its blessings and benefit.

I ask Allāh to bless the children of Islām, and to protect the youth of Islām, to aid them upon memorizing the Qur'ān and understanding the meanings and rulings contained within it.

سُورَةُ الفَاتِحَةِ

Sūrah al-Fātiḥah

Revealed in Mecca

﴿ بِسْمِ اللَّهِ الرَّحْمَٰنِ الرَّحِيمِ ﴿١﴾ الْحَمْدُ لِلَّهِ رَبِّ الْعَالَمِينَ ﴿٢﴾ الرَّحْمَٰنِ الرَّحِيمِ ﴿٣﴾ مَالِكِ يَوْمِ الدِّينِ ﴿٤﴾ إِيَّاكَ نَعْبُدُ وَإِيَّاكَ نَسْتَعِينُ ﴿٥﴾ اهْدِنَا الصِّرَاطَ الْمُسْتَقِيمَ ﴿٦﴾ صِرَاطَ الَّذِينَ أَنْعَمْتَ عَلَيْهِمْ غَيْرِ الْمَغْضُوبِ عَلَيْهِمْ وَلَا الضَّالِّينَ ﴿٧﴾ ﴾

In the Name of Allāh, the Most Beneficent, the Most Merciful. (1) All the praises and thanks belong to Allāh, the Lord of all that exists. (2) The Most Beneficent, the Most Merciful. (3) Sovereign of the Day of Recompense. (4) You (Alone) we worship, and You (Alone) we ask for help. (5) Guide us to the straight path. (6) The path of those upon whom You have bestowed favor, not of those who have evoked Your anger, or of those who are astray. (7)

Explanation

In the Name of Allāh, the Most Beneficent, the Most Merciful. (1)

I seek help upon reciting the Qur'ān, with the Name of Allāh, the Most Beneficent, the Most Merciful.

All the praises and thanks belong to Allāh, the Lord of all that exists. (2) The Most Beneficent, the Most Merciful. (3) Sovereign of the Day of Recompense. (4)

Allāh, He is the God that is worshipped. He is the Lord and the Creator of all the creation. He is the One who bestows mercy upon His slaves. He is the King and Sovereign for the Day of Resurrection.

You (Alone) we worship, and you (Alone) we ask for help. (5)

We worship Allāh, alone. And we seek help from Allāh, alone.

Guide us to the straight path. (6) The path of those upon whom You have bestowed favor,

Guide us to the path of happiness. And the path of happiness is the path of the Prophet ﷺ and his companions.

Not of those who have evoked Your anger, or of those who are astray. (7)

Distance us far away from the deviant paths. These are the paths of the Jews and the Christians.

Lessons from Sūrah al-Fātiḥah

1. Allāh ﷻ is the Creator, the Most Merciful, and the King. Therefore, I love Him, I fear Him, I place my hope in Him. Thus, I worship Him, alone, without partners.

2. Firmness upon the straight path because it is the path of happiness.

سُوْرَةُ الضُّحَىٰ

Sūrah Aḍ-Ḍuḥā

Revealed in Mecca

﴿ وَالضُّحَىٰ ﴿١﴾ وَاللَّيْلِ إِذَا سَجَىٰ ﴿٢﴾ مَا وَدَّعَكَ رَبُّكَ وَمَا قَلَىٰ ﴿٣﴾
وَلَلْآخِرَةُ خَيْرٌ لَّكَ مِنَ الْأُولَىٰ ﴿٤﴾ وَلَسَوْفَ يُعْطِيكَ رَبُّكَ فَتَرْضَىٰ ﴿٥﴾
أَلَمْ يَجِدْكَ يَتِيمًا فَآوَىٰ ﴿٦﴾ وَوَجَدَكَ ضَالًّا فَهَدَىٰ ﴿٧﴾ وَوَجَدَكَ عَائِلًا
فَأَغْنَىٰ ﴿٨﴾ فَأَمَّا الْيَتِيمَ فَلَا تَقْهَرْ ﴿٩﴾ وَأَمَّا السَّائِلَ فَلَا تَنْهَرْ ﴿١٠﴾
وَأَمَّا بِنِعْمَةِ رَبِّكَ فَحَدِّثْ ﴿١١﴾ ﴾

By the forenoon. (1) And by the night when it covers with darkness. (2) Your Lord (O Muḥammad) has neither forsaken you nor hated you. (3) And indeed, the Hereafter is better for you than the present life. (4) And verily, your Lord will give you so that you shall be well-pleased. (5) Did He not find you (O Muḥammad) an orphan and gave you a refuge? (6) And He found you unaware and guided you? (7) And He found you poor and made you self-sufficient. (8) Therefore, treat not the orphan with oppression. (9) And repulse not the beggar. (10) As for the favor of your Lord, then proclaim it. (11)

Explanation

By the forenoon. (1) And by the night when it covers with darkness. (2) Your Lord (O Muḥammad) has neither forsaken you nor hated you. (3) And in-

deed, the Hereafter is better for you than the present life. (4) And verily, your Lord will give you so that you shall be well-pleased. (5)

Allāh ﷻ swore by the day and the night that He did not abandon the Prophet ﷺ, nor is He angry with him. Rather, He will honor him with Paradise, such that he will be well-pleased. And Paradise is much greater than the worldly life.

Did He not find you (O Muḥammad) an orphan and gave you a refuge? (6) And He found you unaware and guided you? (7) And He found you poor and made you self-sufficient. (8)

Allāh ﷻ took care of the Prophet ﷺ in this worldly life when he was a young orphan. He guided him to the laws of Islām and enriched him in his soul and his wealth.

Therefore, treat not the orphan with oppression. (9) And repulse not the beggar. (10) As for the favor of your Lord, then proclaim it. (11)

Do not be harsh toward the child who has lost their father. Do not scold the needy beggar. As for the favors that you have, show gratitude to Allāh ﷻ for them.

Lessons from Sūrah Aḍ-Ḍuḥā

1. Show mercy to the orphans and the poor.
2. Thank Allāh ﷻ for His favors by displaying them without being wasteful.

سُورَةُ الشَّرْحِ

Sūrah ash-Sharḥ

Revealed in Mecca

﴿ أَلَمْ نَشْرَحْ لَكَ صَدْرَكَ ۝١ وَوَضَعْنَا عَنكَ وِزْرَكَ ۝٢ الَّذِي أَنقَضَ
ظَهْرَكَ ۝٣ وَرَفَعْنَا لَكَ ذِكْرَكَ ۝٤ فَإِنَّ مَعَ الْعُسْرِ يُسْرًا ۝٥ إِنَّ مَعَ
الْعُسْرِ يُسْرًا ۝٦ فَإِذَا فَرَغْتَ فَانصَبْ ۝٧ وَإِلَىٰ رَبِّكَ فَارْغَب ۝٨ ﴾

Did We not expand for you (O Muḥammad) your chest? (1) And removed from you your burden (2) Which weighed down your back? (3) And raised high your fame? (4) For indeed, with hardship, there is relief. (5) Indeed, with hardship, there is relief. (6) So when you have finished [your duties], then stand up [for worship]. (7) And to your Lord (Alone) turn your invocations. (8)

Explanation

Did We not expand for you (O Muḥammad) your chest? (1) And removed from you your burden (2) Which weighed down your back? (3) And raised high your fame? (4)

Allāh ﷻ expanded the chest of the Prophet ﷺ with the Qur'ān and Islām. He forgave him of his sins, lightened his burdens, and elevated his reputation.

For indeed, with hardship, there is relief. (5) Indeed, with hardship, there is relief. (6)

Hardship and difficulty go away, and ease and relaxation will come afterward.

So when you have finished [your duties], then stand up [for worship]. (7) And to your Lord (Alone) turn your invocations. (8)

When you have completed your occupation, strive in the worship of your Lord. ﷻ

Lessons from Sūrah Ash-Sharḥ

1. Regardless of how difficult the situation may be, ease is near.
2. Use free time for the worship of Allāh ﷻ.

سُورَةُ التِّينِ

Sūrah at-Tīn

Revealed in Mecca

﴿ وَالتِّينِ وَالزَّيْتُونِ (١) وَطُورِ سِينِينَ (٢) وَهَٰذَا الْبَلَدِ الْأَمِينِ (٣) لَقَدْ
خَلَقْنَا الْإِنسَانَ فِي أَحْسَنِ تَقْوِيمٍ (٤) ثُمَّ رَدَدْنَاهُ أَسْفَلَ سَافِلِينَ (٥) إِلَّا الَّذِينَ
آمَنُوا وَعَمِلُوا الصَّالِحَاتِ فَلَهُمْ أَجْرٌ غَيْرُ مَمْنُونٍ (٦) فَمَا يُكَذِّبُكَ بَعْدُ بِالدِّينِ
(٧) أَلَيْسَ اللَّهُ بِأَحْكَمِ الْحَاكِمِينَ (٨) ﴾

By the fig, and the olive, (1) By Mount Sinai, (2) And by this secure city, (3) We have certainly created man in the best of stature; (4) then We reduced him to the lowest of the low, (5) Except for those who believe and do righteous deeds, for they will have a reward uninterrupted. (6) Then what causes you to deny the Day of Resurrection? (7) Is not Allāh the Best of judges? (8)

Explanation

By the fig, and the olive, (1) By Mount Sinai, (2) And by this secure city, (3)

Allāh ﷻ swore by the plants, the fig and the olive, and mount Sinai, the mount Prophet Mūsā عليه السلام was at when Allāh ﷻ spoke to him. And by the secure city of Mecca, the city in which Allāh ﷻ sent down revelation to Prophet Muḥammad ﷺ.

We have certainly created man in the best of stature; (4) then We reduced him to the lowest of the low, (5) Except for those who believe and do righteous deeds, for they will have a reward uninterrupted. (6)

Allāh ﷻ swore that He created mankind in the best form in this worldly life. If he does not believe in Allāh, and he does not do righteous actions, in the Hereafter he will return to the lowest position and the most hideous form. The believers who perform righteous actions will be in Paradise. The bliss of Paradise will never be interrupted, its splendor will never come to an end.

Then what causes you to deny the Day of Resurrection? (7) Is not Allāh the Best of judges? (8)

Why O mankind, do you disbelieve in the Day of Judgment? Do you not know that Allāh ﷻ is a Just and Fair Ruler? He does not create the creation without purpose; rather, He will raise them from the dead and recompense them.

Lessons from Sūrah at-Tīn

1. Allāh ﷻ honored mankind and created him with the best form and body.
2. The true value of man is found in his faith and righteous actions.

سُوْرَةُ العَلَقِ

Sūrah al-'Alaq

Revealed in Mecca

﴿ اقْرَأْ بِاسْمِ رَبِّكَ الَّذِي خَلَقَ (١) خَلَقَ الْإِنسَانَ مِنْ عَلَقٍ (٢) اقْرَأْ وَرَبُّكَ
الْأَكْرَمُ (٣) الَّذِي عَلَّمَ بِالْقَلَمِ (٤) عَلَّمَ الْإِنسَانَ مَا لَمْ يَعْلَمْ (٥) كَلَّا إِنَّ
الْإِنسَانَ لَيَطْغَىٰ (٦) أَن رَّآهُ اسْتَغْنَىٰ (٧) إِنَّ إِلَىٰ رَبِّكَ الرُّجْعَىٰ (٨)
أَرَأَيْتَ الَّذِي يَنْهَىٰ (٩) عَبْدًا إِذَا صَلَّىٰ (١٠) أَرَأَيْتَ إِن كَانَ عَلَى الْهُدَىٰ
(١١) أَوْ أَمَرَ بِالتَّقْوَىٰ (١٢) أَرَأَيْتَ إِن كَذَّبَ وَتَوَلَّىٰ (١٣) أَلَمْ يَعْلَم بِأَنَّ اللَّهَ
يَرَىٰ (١٤) كَلَّا لَئِن لَّمْ يَنتَهِ لَنَسْفَعًا بِالنَّاصِيَةِ (١٥) نَاصِيَةٍ كَاذِبَةٍ خَاطِئَةٍ
(١٦) فَلْيَدْعُ نَادِيَهُ (١٧) سَنَدْعُ الزَّبَانِيَةَ (١٨) كَلَّا لَا تُطِعْهُ وَاسْجُدْ وَاقْتَرِب
۩ (١٩) ﴾

Recite in the name of your Lord who created (1) He created man from a clot. (2) Recite, and your Lord is the most Generous, (3) The One Who taught by the pen. (4) He taught man that which he knew not. (5) No! But indeed, man transgresses all bounds (6) Because he considers himself self-sufficient. (7) Indeed, to your Lord is the return. (8) Have you seen the one who prevents (9) A servant when he prays? (10) Have you seen if he is upon guidance (11) Or enjoins piety? (12) Have you seen if he denies and turns away? (13) Does he not know that Allāh sees? (14) No! If he does not desist, We will surely drag him by the forelock, (15) A lying, sinning forelock. (16) Then, let him call upon his council of helpers. (17) We will call the guards of Hell. (18) Nay! Do not obey him. Fall prostrate and draw near to Allāh! (19)

Explanation

Recite in the name of your Lord who created (1) He created man from a clot. (2) Recite, and your Lord is the most Generous, (3) The One Who taught by the pen. (4) He taught man that which he knew not. (5)

Recite the Qur'ān O Muḥammad, seeking the help of Allāh ﷻ, the One Who created man. He is the Most Generous. He taught mankind how to write. And He taught man that which man did not know.

No! But indeed, man transgresses all bounds (6) Because he considers himself self-sufficient. (7) Indeed, to your Lord is the return. (8)

Man transgresses the laws of Allāh ﷻ, and he becomes arrogant if his wealth increases; even though he will return to Allāh, and Allāh ﷻ will take him to account for his actions.

Have you seen the one who prevents (9) A servant when he prays? (10) Have you seen if he is upon guidance (11) Or enjoins piety? (12) Have you seen if he denies and turns away? (13) Does he not know that Allāh sees? (14)

This verse refers to a man named Abū Jahl the liar, who did not believe in Allāh ﷻ and prevented the Prophet ﷺ from prayer, although the Prophet ﷺ was rightly guided and pious. Allāh ﷻ observed what he did, and He will take him to account for it.

No! If he does not desist, We will surely drag him by the forelock, (15) A lying, sinning forelock. (16) Then, let him call upon his council of helpers. (17) We will call the guards of Hell. (18) Nay! Do not obey him. Fall prostrate and draw near to Allāh! (19)

Allāh ﷻ will seize Abū Jahl by his head and throw him into the Hellfire. If he calls upon his council to help him, Allāh ﷻ will send against him the angels of the Hellfire to seize him at that moment.

Lessons from Sūrah Al-'Alaq

1. The importance of knowledge, reading, and writing.
2. Do not harm those who are praying, nor prevent them from praying or mock them.

سُورَةُ الْقَدْرِ

Sūrah al-Qadr

Revealed in Madinah

﴿ إِنَّا أَنزَلْنَاهُ فِي لَيْلَةِ الْقَدْرِ ﴿١﴾ وَمَا أَدْرَاكَ مَا لَيْلَةُ الْقَدْرِ ﴿٢﴾ لَيْلَةُ الْقَدْرِ
خَيْرٌ مِّنْ أَلْفِ شَهْرٍ ﴿٣﴾ تَنَزَّلُ الْمَلَائِكَةُ وَالرُّوحُ فِيهَا بِإِذْنِ رَبِّهِم مِّن كُلِّ
أَمْرٍ ﴿٤﴾ سَلَامٌ هِيَ حَتَّىٰ مَطْلَعِ الْفَجْرِ ﴿٥﴾ ﴾

Indeed, We sent it (this Qur'ān) down in the night of Decree. (1) And what can make you know what is the Night of Decree? (2) The Night of Decree is better than a thousand months. (3) The angels and the Spirit descend therein, by permission of their Lord, for every matter. (4) Peace it is until the emergence of dawn. (5)

Explanation

Allāh ﷻ sent down the Qur'ān during the month of Ramaḍān, on the Night of Decree. This one night is better than 85 years of a person's life. This is the night wherein the angels descend, along with the angel Jibrīl, with mercy and peace until the dawn enters.

Lessons from Sūrah al-Qadr

1. The greatness of the Night of Decree, so I will strive diligently in worship.
2. I will be diligent upon reciting the Qur'ān, especially during the month of Ramaḍān.

سُورَةُ الْبَيِّنَةِ

Sūrah al-Bayyinah

Revealed in Madinah

﴿ لَمْ يَكُنِ الَّذِينَ كَفَرُوا مِنْ أَهْلِ الْكِتَابِ وَالْمُشْرِكِينَ مُنفَكِّينَ حَتَّىٰ تَأْتِيَهُمُ
الْبَيِّنَةُ (١) رَسُولٌ مِّنَ اللَّهِ يَتْلُو صُحُفًا مُّطَهَّرَةً (٢) فِيهَا كُتُبٌ قَيِّمَةٌ (٣)
وَمَا تَفَرَّقَ الَّذِينَ أُوتُوا الْكِتَابَ إِلَّا مِن بَعْدِ مَا جَاءَتْهُمُ الْبَيِّنَةُ (٤) وَمَا أُمِرُوا
إِلَّا لِيَعْبُدُوا اللَّهَ مُخْلِصِينَ لَهُ الدِّينَ حُنَفَاءَ وَيُقِيمُوا الصَّلَاةَ وَيُؤْتُوا الزَّكَاةَ ۚ
وَذَٰلِكَ دِينُ الْقَيِّمَةِ (٥) إِنَّ الَّذِينَ كَفَرُوا مِنْ أَهْلِ الْكِتَابِ وَالْمُشْرِكِينَ فِي نَارِ
جَهَنَّمَ خَالِدِينَ فِيهَا ۚ أُولَٰئِكَ هُمْ شَرُّ الْبَرِيَّةِ (٦) إِنَّ الَّذِينَ آمَنُوا وَعَمِلُوا
الصَّالِحَاتِ أُولَٰئِكَ هُمْ خَيْرُ الْبَرِيَّةِ (٧) جَزَاؤُهُمْ عِندَ رَبِّهِمْ جَنَّاتُ عَدْنٍ
تَجْرِي مِن تَحْتِهَا الْأَنْهَارُ خَالِدِينَ فِيهَا أَبَدًا ۖ رَّضِيَ اللَّهُ عَنْهُمْ وَرَضُوا عَنْهُ ۚ
ذَٰلِكَ لِمَنْ خَشِيَ رَبَّهُ (٨) ﴾

Those who disbelieved among the People of the Scripture and the polytheists were not going to leave (their disbelief) until there came to them clear evidence. (1) A Messenger from Allāh, reciting purified scriptures (2) Containing correct writings. (3) Nor did those who were given the Scripture become divided until after there had come to them clear evidence. (4) And they were not commanded except to worship Allāh, [being] sincere to Him in religion, inclining to truth, and to establish prayer and give charity. And that is the correct religion. (5) Verily, those who disbelieve from among the people of the Scripture (Jews and Christians), and the polytheists, will abide in the Fire of Hell. They are the worst of creatures. (6) Verily, those who believe and do righteous good deeds, they are the best of creatures. (7) Their reward with Allāh will be gardens of perpetual residence beneath which rivers flow, wherein they will abide forever, Allāh being pleased with them, and they with Him. That is for whoever has feared his Lord. (8)

Explanation

Those who disbelieved among the People of the Scripture and the polytheists were not going to leave (their disbelief) until there came to them clear evidence, (1) A Messenger from Allāh, reciting purified scriptures (2) Containing correct writings (3).

The Jews, Christians, and polytheists were not going to leave the misguidance they were upon until the Prophet ﷺ came to them with the Qur'ān, which is purified from falsehood, and contains correct laws.

Nor did those who were given the Scripture become divided until after there had come to them clear evidence. (4) And they were not commanded except to worship Allāh, [being] sincere to Him in religion, inclining to truth, and to establish prayer and give charity. And that is the correct religion. (5)

The People of the Scripture (Jews and Christians) divided regarding belief in the Prophet ﷺ. Some of them believed in him, and some of them disbelieved in him. And how could they disbelieve in him when he came with the upright religion, making the religion sincere for Allāh ﷻ, establishing the prayer and giving charity?!

Verily, those who disbelieve from among the people of the Scripture (Jews and Christians), and the polytheists, will abide in the Fire of Hell. They are the worst of creatures. (6) Verily, those who believe and do righteous good deeds, they are the best of creatures. (7) Their reward with Allāh will be gardens of perpetual residence beneath which rivers flow, wherein they will abide forever, Allāh being pleased with them, and they with Him. That is for whoever has feared his Lord. (8)

The recompense of those who disbelieve in the Prophet ﷺ is the Hell-fire. The reward for those who believe in Allāh ﷻ and fear Him, follow the Messenger ﷺ, and do righteous actions, is Paradise.

Lessons from Sūrah al-Bayyinah

1. Islām, its laws and rulings are tolerant and principled.
2. The person who believes in Allāh ﷻ, follows the Messenger ﷺ, and does righteous actions, Allāh is pleased with them, and He will enter them into Paradise.

سُورَةُ الزَّلْزَلَةِ

Sūrah az-Zalzalah

Revealed in Madinah

﴿ إِذَا زُلْزِلَتِ الْأَرْضُ زِلْزَالَهَا ﴿١﴾ وَأَخْرَجَتِ الْأَرْضُ أَثْقَالَهَا ﴿٢﴾ وَقَالَ
الْإِنسَانُ مَا لَهَا ﴿٣﴾ يَوْمَئِذٍ تُحَدِّثُ أَخْبَارَهَا ﴿٤﴾ بِأَنَّ رَبَّكَ أَوْحَىٰ لَهَا ﴿٥﴾
يَوْمَئِذٍ يَصْدُرُ النَّاسُ أَشْتَاتًا لِّيُرَوْا أَعْمَالَهُمْ ﴿٦﴾ فَمَن يَعْمَلْ مِثْقَالَ ذَرَّةٍ خَيْرًا
يَرَهُ ﴿٧﴾ وَمَن يَعْمَلْ مِثْقَالَ ذَرَّةٍ شَرًّا يَرَهُ ﴿٨﴾ ﴾

When the earth is shaken with its (final) earthquake, (1) And when the earth throws out its burdens, (2) And man will say, "What is the matter with it?" (3) That Day, it will declare its information (4) Because your Lord has inspired it. (5) That Day, mankind will proceed in scattered groups to be shown their deeds. (6) So, whosoever does good equal to the weight of an atom shall see it, (7) And whosoever does evil equal to the weight of an atom shall see it. (8)

Explanation

When the earth is shaken with its (final) earthquake, (1) And when the earth throws out its burdens, (2) And man will say, "What is the matter with it?" (3) That Day, it will declare its information (4) Because your Lord has inspired it. (5)

The earth will shake violently on the Day of Judgment. The earth will expel the deceased upon its surface. The people will be terrified and say, "What is the matter with it?!" On that day, Allāh ﷻ will command the earth to divulge everything the people did upon the earth.

That Day, mankind will proceed in scattered groups to be shown their deeds. (6) So, whosoever does good equal to the weight of an atom shall see it, (7) And whosoever does evil equal to the weight of an atom shall see it. (8)

On the Day of Judgment, after the reckoning, the people will go to be shown their deeds that they did in this life. They will even be shown their small actions. Whoever did good will see good and delight. Whoever did evil will see evil and punishment.

Lessons from Sūrah az-Zalzalah

1. Fear of the Day of Judgment, because of its great terrors.
2. Diligence upon good deeds, even if they are small, while avoiding evil deeds, even if they are small.

سُورَةُ الْعَادِيَاتِ

Sūrah al-'Ādiyāt

Revealed in Mecca

﴿وَٱلْعَٰدِيَٰتِ ضَبْحًا ﴿١﴾ فَٱلْمُورِيَٰتِ قَدْحًا ﴿٢﴾ فَٱلْمُغِيرَٰتِ صُبْحًا ﴿٣﴾
فَأَثَرْنَ بِهِۦ نَقْعًا ﴿٤﴾ فَوَسَطْنَ بِهِۦ جَمْعًا ﴿٥﴾ إِنَّ ٱلْإِنسَٰنَ لِرَبِّهِۦ لَكَنُودٌ ﴿٦﴾
وَإِنَّهُۥ عَلَىٰ ذَٰلِكَ لَشَهِيدٌ ﴿٧﴾ وَإِنَّهُۥ لِحُبِّ ٱلْخَيْرِ لَشَدِيدٌ ﴿٨﴾ ۞ أَفَلَا يَعْلَمُ إِذَا
بُعْثِرَ مَا فِى ٱلْقُبُورِ ﴿٩﴾ وَحُصِّلَ مَا فِى ٱلصُّدُورِ ﴿١٠﴾ إِنَّ رَبَّهُم بِهِمْ يَوْمَئِذٍ
لَّخَبِيرٌۢ ﴿١١﴾﴾

By the (steeds) that run, with panting, (1) Striking sparks of fire (by their hooves), (2) And scouring to the raid at dawn, (3) Stirring up clouds of dust, (4) And penetrating forthwith as one into the midst (of the foe); (5) Verily, man is ungrateful to his Lord, (6) And to that he bears witness. (7) And verily, he is violent in the love of wealth. (8) Knows he not that when the contents of the graves are poured forth, (9) And that which is in the breasts (of men) is made known, (10) Verily, that Day, their Lord is Fully Acquainted with them. (11)

Explanation

By the (steeds) that run, with panting, (1) Striking sparks of fire (by their hooves), (2) And scouring to the raid at dawn, (3) Stirring up clouds of dust, (4) And penetrating forthwith as one into the midst (of the foe); (5) Verily, man is ungrateful to his Lord, (6) And to that he bears witness. (7) And verily, he is violent in the love of wealth. (8)

Allāh ﷻ swore by the stallions because of their beauty, speed, and strength, that man denies the favors of his Lord; although man is a witness against himself, and obsessive with his love of wealth.

Knows he not that when the contents of the graves are poured forth, (9) And that which is in the breasts (of men) is made known, (10) Verily, that Day, their Lord is Fully Acquainted with them. (11)

Man knows that he will die, and then he will be raised from his grave. Allāh ﷻ will reveal everything within the hearts of man from good and evil, because Allāh ﷻ has full knowledge of man and what his heart contains.

Lessons from Sūrah al-'Ādiyāt

1. To be generous with my wealth and not stingy.
2. Rectify my heart because Allāh ﷻ is looking at it. And He will reveal what is in it from good or evil.

سُورَةُ ٱلْقَارِعَةِ

Sūrah al-Qāri‘ah

Revealed in Mecca

﴿ ٱلۡقَارِعَةُ ١ مَا ٱلۡقَارِعَةُ ٢ وَمَآ أَدۡرَىٰكَ مَا ٱلۡقَارِعَةُ ٣ يَوۡمَ
يَكُونُ ٱلنَّاسُ كَٱلۡفَرَاشِ ٱلۡمَبۡثُوثِ ٤ وَتَكُونُ ٱلۡجِبَالُ كَٱلۡعِهۡنِ ٱلۡمَنفُوشِ
٥ فَأَمَّا مَن ثَقُلَتۡ مَوَٰزِينُهُۥ ٦ فَهُوَ فِي عِيشَةٖ رَّاضِيَةٖ ٧ وَأَمَّا
مَنۡ خَفَّتۡ مَوَٰزِينُهُۥ ٨ فَأُمُّهُۥ هَاوِيَةٞ ٩ وَمَآ أَدۡرَىٰكَ مَا هِيَهۡ ١٠
نَارٌ حَامِيَةُۢ ١١ ﴾

The Striking Calamity, (1) What is the Striking Calamity? (2) And what can make you know what is the Striking Calamity? (3) It is the Day when people will be like moths scattered about, (4) And the mountains will be like carded wool. (5) Then, as for one whose scales are heavy [with good deeds], (6) He will be in a pleasant life. (7) But as for one whose scales are light, (8) His refuge will be an abyss. (9) And what can make you know what that is? (10) It is a fiercely blazing Fire! (11)

Explanation

The Striking Calamity, (1) What is the Striking Calamity? (2) And what can make you know what is the Striking Calamity? (3) It is the Day when people will be like moths scattered about, (4) And the mountains will be like carded wool. (5)

The Day of Judgement, it is the day when the hearts will shake with fear due to the terror on that day. The fear will cause the people to scatter about senselessly, like dispersed moths. The huge mountains will crumble like flakey wool.

Then, as for one whose scales are heavy [with good deeds], (6) He will be in a pleasant life. (7) But as for one whose scales are light, (8) His refuge will be an abyss. (9) And what can make you know what that is? (10) It is a fiercely blazing Fire! (11)

The people will be divided into categories on the Day of Judgment with regard to their scales of deeds. Those who will be happy are the people whose good deeds outweigh their evil deeds. They will enter Paradise. Those who will be miserable are those whose sins outweigh their good deeds. They will fall upon their heads into the blazing fire of Hell.

Lessons from Sūrah al-Qāri'ah

1. The Day of Judgment will have great terror and fear, so I must prepare myself for it.
2. I will do righteous deeds to make my scale of good deeds heavy. I will not commit sins, because this would make my scale of good deeds light.

سُورَةُ ٱلتَّكَاثُرِ

Sūrah at-Takāthur

Revealed in Mecca

﴿ أَلْهَىٰكُمُ ٱلتَّكَاثُرُ ۝١ حَتَّىٰ زُرْتُمُ ٱلْمَقَابِرَ ۝٢ كَلَّا سَوْفَ تَعْلَمُونَ ۝٣ ثُمَّ
كَلَّا سَوْفَ تَعْلَمُونَ ۝٤ كَلَّا لَوْ تَعْلَمُونَ عِلْمَ ٱلْيَقِينِ ۝٥ لَتَرَوُنَّ ٱلْجَحِيمَ
۝٦ ثُمَّ لَتَرَوُنَّهَا عَيْنَ ٱلْيَقِينِ ۝٧ ثُمَّ لَتُسْـَٔلُنَّ يَوْمَئِذٍ عَنِ ٱلنَّعِيمِ ۝٨ ﴾

The mutual rivalry (for worldly things) diverts you, (1) Until you visit the graves. (2) Nay! You shall come to know! (3) Again nay! You shall come to know! (4) Nay! If you knew with a sure knowledge, (5) Verily, you shall see the blazing Fire! (6) And again, you shall see it with certainty of sight! (7) Then on that Day, you shall be asked about the delights! (8)

Explanation

The mutual rivalry (for worldly things) diverts you, (1) Until you visit the graves. (2) Nay! You shall come to know! (3) Again nay! You shall come to know! (4) Nay! If you knew with a sure knowledge, (5)

This worldly life diverts the people from the Hereafter, until they die and then enter the grave. If they have knowledge, this temporary world would not distract them from the permanent Afterlife.

Verily, you shall see the blazing Fire! (6) And again, you shall see it with certainty of sight! (7) Then on that Day, you shall be asked about the delights! (8)

Due to their lack of knowledge, their hearts are heedless. Then on the Day of Judgment, they will surely see the Hellfire with their eyes. They will be questioned about the favors Allāh ﷻ bestowed upon them in this worldly life.

Lessons from Sūrah at-Takāthur

1. Do not allow myself to be distracted from the Hereafter by those things that do not benefit me.
2. I will show gratitude for the favors of Allāh ﷻ, and I will use these favors in a way He loves.

سُورَةُ ٱلْعَصْرِ

Sūrah al-ʻAṣr

Revealed in Mecca

﴿وَٱلۡعَصۡرِ ١ إِنَّ ٱلۡإِنسَٰنَ لَفِي خُسۡرٍ ٢ إِلَّا ٱلَّذِينَ ءَامَنُواْ وَعَمِلُواْ
ٱلصَّٰلِحَٰتِ وَتَوَاصَوۡاْ بِٱلۡحَقِّ وَتَوَاصَوۡاْ بِٱلصَّبۡرِ ٣﴾

By time, (1) Indeed, mankind is in loss, (2) Except for those who have believed and do righteous deeds, and advise each other to truth, and advise each other to patience. (3)

Explanation

Allāh ﷻ swears by the time, due to its great importance, that all mankind is in a state of loss in this life and the Hereafter, except for those who adorn themselves with four qualities.

1. Belief in Allāh ﷻ, His angels, His Books, His messengers, the Day of Judgment, and divine decree.
2. Perform righteous actions that are obligatory and recommended.
3. Invite to the true religion.
4. Show patience upon the obedience of Allāh ﷻ, patience in avoiding sins, and patience with the decree of Allāh ﷻ.

Lessons from Sūrah al-'Aṣr

1. The importance of time in my life.
2. I will be diligent in seeking knowledge so I can know the qualities that will save me from loss.

سُورَةُ ٱلْهُمَزَةِ

Sūrah al-Humazah

Revealed in Mecca

﴿وَيْلٌ لِّكُلِّ هُمَزَةٍ لُّمَزَةٍ ۝١ ٱلَّذِى جَمَعَ مَالًا وَعَدَّدَهُۥ ۝٢ يَحْسَبُ أَنَّ مَالَهُۥٓ
أَخْلَدَهُۥ ۝٣ كَلَّا ۖ لَيُنۢبَذَنَّ فِى ٱلْحُطَمَةِ ۝٤ وَمَآ أَدْرَىٰكَ مَا ٱلْحُطَمَةُ ۝٥
نَارُ ٱللَّهِ ٱلْمُوقَدَةُ ۝٦ ٱلَّتِى تَطَّلِعُ عَلَى ٱلْأَفْـِٔدَةِ ۝٧ إِنَّهَا عَلَيْهِم مُّؤْصَدَةٌ
۝٨ فِى عَمَدٍ مُّمَدَّدَةٍۭ ۝٩﴾

Woe to every slanderer and backbiter (1) Who has gathered wealth and counted it. (2) He thinks his wealth will make him immortal. (3) No! He will surely be thrown into the crushing Fire. (4) And what can make you know what is the crushing Fire? (5) It is the fire of Allāh, kindled, (6) Which leaps up over the hearts. (7) Indeed, Hellfire will be closed down upon them (8) In pillars stretched forth. (9)

Explanation

Woe to every slanderer and backbiter (1) Who has gathered wealth and counted it. (2) He thinks his wealth will make him immortal. (3)

There is a severe punishment for those who harm, slander, and backbite the believers, and those who think their wealth will allow them to live in this world forever.

(4) And what can make you know what is the crushing Fire? (5) It is the fire of Allāh, kindled, (6) Which leaps up over the hearts. (7) Indeed, Hellfire will be closed down upon them (8) In pillars stretched forth. (9)

On the contrary, his wealth will not allow him to live in this world forever; rather, Allāh ﷻ will throw him in the Hellfire, the fire that crushes everything that is thrown in it; the fire kindled by Allāh. It is severe in its heat. Its pain touches the hearts. It will be enclosed over them with pillars they cannot escape from.

Lessons from Sūrah al-Humazah

1. I will not mock, slander, or ridicule the people.
2. I will do every good deed I can to distance myself from the Hellfire because it is extremely hot.

سُورَةُ الْفِيلِ

Sūrah al-Fīl

Revealed in Mecca

﴿ أَلَمْ تَرَ كَيْفَ فَعَلَ رَبُّكَ بِأَصْحَٰبِ ٱلْفِيلِ ﴿١﴾ أَلَمْ يَجْعَلْ كَيْدَهُمْ فِى تَضْلِيلٍ
﴿٢﴾ وَأَرْسَلَ عَلَيْهِمْ طَيْرًا أَبَابِيلَ ﴿٣﴾ تَرْمِيهِم بِحِجَارَةٍ مِّن سِجِّيلٍ ﴿٤﴾
فَجَعَلَهُمْ كَعَصْفٍ مَّأْكُولٍ ﴿٥﴾ ﴾

Have you not considered how your Lord dealt with the companions of the elephant? (1) Did He not make their plot go astray? (2) And He sent against them birds, in flocks, (3) Striking them with stones of baked clay. (4) And He made them like eaten straw. (5)

Explanation

Do you not know, O Muḥammad, that Allāh ﷻ, with His Might, repelled the companions of the elephant—Abraha and his people—when they wanted to destroy the Ka'bah? Thus, He sent against them many birds carrying rigid, strong stones, throwing them at the companions of the elephants until they became like straw that had been eaten by animals and then trampled over.

Lessons from Sūrah al-Fīl

1. Allāh protects His religion and His house, the Ka'bah.
2. Everyone who opposes the religion of Allāh ﷻ will be defeated and destroyed.

سُورَةُ قُرَيْشٍ

Sūrah Quraysh

Revealed in Mecca

﴿ لِإِيلَٰفِ قُرَيْشٍ
﴿١﴾ إِۦلَٰفِهِمْ رِحْلَةَ ٱلشِّتَآءِ وَٱلصَّيْفِ ﴿٢﴾ فَلْيَعْبُدُوا۟ رَبَّ هَٰذَا ٱلْبَيْتِ ﴿٣﴾ ٱلَّذِىٓ أَ
طْعَمَهُم مِّن جُوعٍ وَءَامَنَهُم مِّنْ خَوْفٍۭ ﴿٤﴾ ﴾

For the security of the Quraysh, (1) Their security in the caravan of winter and summer, (2) Let them worship the Lord of this House, (3) Who has fed them [saving them from hunger], and made them safe from fear. (4)

Explanation

Allāh ﷻ bestowed favors upon the tribe of Quraysh by making it easy for them to travel for business and trade. During the winter, they would travel to Yemen. During the summer, they would travel to the area of Syria-Palestine. Therefore, it is obligatory upon them to worship Allāh ﷻ, alone, because He is the One who favored them with this blessing. He is the One who fed them and kept them safe in these lands.

Lessons from Sūrah Quraysh

1. Worship is only for Allāh ﷻ, alone.
2. Enjoying a good livelihood and safety are blessings. And we must show gratitude to Allāh ﷻ for these blessings.

سُوْرَةُ الْمَاعُون

Sūrah al-Mā‘ūn

Revealed in Mecca

﴿ أَرَءَيْتَ ٱلَّذِى يُكَذِّبُ بِٱلدِّينِ ﴿١﴾ فَذَٰلِكَ ٱلَّذِى يَدُعُّ ٱلْيَتِيمَ ﴿٢﴾ وَلَا يَحُضُّ
عَلَىٰ طَعَامِ ٱلْمِسْكِينِ ﴿٣﴾ فَوَيْلٌ لِّلْمُصَلِّينَ ﴿٤﴾ ٱلَّذِينَ هُمْ عَن صَلَاتِهِمْ
سَاهُونَ ﴿٥﴾ ٱلَّذِينَ هُمْ يُرَآءُونَ ﴿٦﴾ وَيَمْنَعُونَ ٱلْمَاعُونَ ﴿٧﴾ ﴾

Have you seen him who denies the Recompense? (1) This is the one who pushes away the orphan (2) And does not encourage feeding the poor. (3) So, woe to those who pray, (4) Those who delay their prayers, (5) Those who do good deeds only to be seen (of men), (6) And prevent small acts of kindnesses. (7)

Explanation

Have you seen him who denies the Recompense? (1) This is the one who pushes away the orphan (2) And does not encourage feeding the poor. (3)

Those who deny the Day of Judgment, their manners become horrible. They oppress the orphans, and they do not feed the poor and needy.

So, woe to those who pray, (4) Those who delay their prayers, (5) Those who do good deeds only to be seen (of men), (6) And prevent small acts of kindnesses. (7)

There is a severe punishment for those who do not pray the prayers during the proper times, or they leave off the pillars of the prayer. These are the people who pray seeking the praise of men. And because they are stingy, they refuse to give even a small amount of kindness.

Lessons from Sūrah Al-Mā'ūn

1. Corrupt beliefs result in corrupt actions.
2. The importance of establishing the prayer with its conditions and pillars.

سُورَةُ الْكَوْثَرِ

Sūrah al-Kawthar

Revealed in Mecca

﴿ إِنَّآ أَعْطَيْنَٰكَ ٱلْكَوْثَرَ ۝١ فَصَلِّ لِرَبِّكَ وَٱنْحَرْ ۝٢ إِنَّ شَانِئَكَ هُوَ ٱلْأَبْتَرُ ۝٣ ﴾

Indeed, We have granted you [O Muḥammad] al-Kawthar. (1) So, pray to your Lord and sacrifice to Him alone. (2) Indeed, your enemy will be one cut off. (3)

Explanation

Allāh ﷻ gave the Prophet ﷺ a great river in Paradise. Its taste is sweeter than honey, its color is whiter than snow, its edges are gold and silver; inside of it are rubies and pearls. Therefore, pray, O Muḥammad, to your Lord, alone, and sacrifice to Him alone, because He is the Creator, the One who bestows favors. As for the one who hates you and shows animosity toward you, he will be debased and cut off from good.

Lessons from Sūrah al-Kawthar

1. Those who obey the Messenger of Allāh ﷺ will drink from the river of the Messenger of Allāh ﷺ.
2. My worship, all of it, is exclusively for Allāh, alone.

سُورَةُ الْكَافِرُونَ

Sūrah al-Kāfirūn

Revealed in Mecca

﴿ قُلْ يَـٰٓأَيُّهَا ٱلْكَـٰفِرُونَ ۝١ لَآ أَعْبُدُ مَا تَعْبُدُونَ ۝٢ وَلَآ أَنتُمْ عَـٰبِدُونَ مَآ أَعْبُدُ
۝٣ وَلَآ أَنَا۠ عَابِدٌ مَّا عَبَدتُّمْ ۝٤ وَلَآ أَنتُمْ عَـٰبِدُونَ مَآ أَعْبُدُ ۝٥ لَكُمْ دِينُكُمْ
وَلِىَ دِينِ ۝٦ ﴾

Say, "O disbelievers, (1) I do not worship what you worship. (2) Nor are you worshippers of what I worship. (3) Nor will I be a worshipper of what you worship. (4) Nor will you be worshippers of what I worship. (5) For you is your religion, and for me is my religion." (6)

Explanation

Allāh ﷻ commanded His Prophet ﷺ to say to the disbelievers, with certainty and emphasis, that he does not worship anyone other than Allāh, and that the disbelievers do not worship Allāh ﷻ. This is because they worship Allah, but they associate partner with Him in their worship. Therefore, for them is their religion, which is polytheism; and for him is the religion of Islām, which is monotheism.

Lessons from Sūrah al-Kāfirūn

1. I free myself from polytheism, and I warn against it.
2. I must not abandon my religion or waiver in it; rather, I must hold firmly to it until I die.

سُورَةُ النَّصْرِ

Sūrah an-Naṣr

Revealed in Madinah

﴿ إِذَا جَآءَ نَصۡرُ ٱللَّهِ وَٱلۡفَتۡحُ ١ وَرَأَيۡتَ ٱلنَّاسَ يَدۡخُلُونَ فِى دِينِ ٱللَّهِ أَفۡوَاجٗا
٢ فَسَبِّحۡ بِحَمۡدِ رَبِّكَ وَٱسۡتَغۡفِرۡهُۚ إِنَّهُۥ كَانَ تَوَّابَۢا ٣ ﴾

When the victory of Allāh has come and the conquest, (1) And you see the people entering the religion of Allāh in crowds, (2) Then glorify the Praises of your Lord and ask His Forgiveness. Verily, He is the One Who accepts the repentance and Who forgives. (3)

Explanation

When the help of Allāh ﷻ comes to the Prophet ﷺ, and the Muslims against their enemies, and Mecca is conquered, and you see the people entering Islām in large groups, then it is upon you, O Muḥammad, to glorify Allāh ﷻ, praise Him, and seek His forgiveness; because Allāh accepts the repentance of His slaves constantly, and His forgiveness is great.

Lessons from Sūrah an-Naṣr

1. If the Muslims help in the cause of Allāh ﷻ, it is inevitable that Allāh ﷻ will send His help to the Muslims.
2. The people must seek Allāh's forgiveness because the slave makes mistakes, while the Lord ﷻ forgives.

سُورَةُ المَسَدِ

Sūrah al-Masad

Revealed in Madinah

﴿ تَبَّتْ يَدَآ أَبِى لَهَبٍ وَتَبَّ ﴿١﴾ مَآ أَغْنَىٰ عَنْهُ مَالُهُۥ وَمَا كَسَبَ ﴿٢﴾
سَيَصْلَىٰ نَارًا ذَاتَ لَهَبٍ ﴿٣﴾ وَٱمْرَأَتُهُۥ حَمَّالَةَ ٱلْحَطَبِ ﴿٤﴾ فِى جِيدِهَا حَبْلٌ
مِّن مَّسَدٍۭ ﴿٥﴾ ﴾

May the hands of Abū Lahab be ruined, and ruined is he. (1) His wealth and his children will not benefit him! (2) He will be burnt in a Fire of blazing flames! (3) And his wife as well—the carrier of firewood. (4) Around her neck is a rope of twisted fiber. (5)

Explanation

May the hands of Abū Lahab be ruined, and ruined is he. (1) His wealth and his children will not benefit him! (2) He will be burnt in a Fire of blazing flames! (3)

The paternal uncle of the Prophet ﷺ was destroyed. He suffered a great loss due to his animosity toward the Prophet ﷺ. His wealth will not help him at all against the punishment of Allāh ﷻ. He will be burnt in a fire that has tremendous burning flames.

And his wife as well—the carrier of firewood. (4) Around her neck is a rope of twisted fiber. (5)

Umm Jamīl, the wife of Abū Lahab, used to assist her husband in harming the Prophet ﷺ. Thus, her recompense will be that she will have a twisted rope of fiber around her neck in the Hellfire, along with her husband.

Lessons from Sūrah al-Masad

1. The lineage of an individual will not benefit him if he wars against Islām.
2. Do not help people do evil, even if they are your closest relatives.

سُوْرَةُ الإِخْلَاصِ

Sūrah al-'Ikhlāṣ

Revealed in Mecca

﴿ قُلْ هُوَ ٱللَّهُ أَحَدٌ ﴿١﴾ ٱللَّهُ ٱلصَّمَدُ ﴿٢﴾ لَمْ يَلِدْ وَلَمْ يُولَدْ ﴿٣﴾ وَلَمْ يَكُن لَّهُۥ
كُفُوًا أَحَدٌۢ ﴿٤﴾ ﴾

Say, "He is Allāh, [who is] One, (1) Allāh, the Eternal Refuge. (2) He begets not, nor was He begotten. (3) And there is none co-equal or comparable to Him." (4)

Explanation

Allāh ﷻ, He is the One true deity, the object of worship, and He has no partners. He is the One to Whom the creation turns for all their needs. From the perfection of the Oneness of Allāh is He has no parents and no children. And from His perfection is, there is nothing that resembles Him.

Lessons from Sūrah al-'Ikhlāṣ

1. To worship Allāh ﷻ, alone, because He is the One who created me and provides for me.
2. Allāh is perfect and complete in His Names and Attributes.

سُورَةُ الْفَلَقِ

Sūrah al-Falaq

Revealed in Madinah

﴿قُلْ أَعُوذُ بِرَبِّ ٱلْفَلَقِ ۝١ مِن شَرِّ مَا خَلَقَ ۝٢ وَمِن شَرِّ غَاسِقٍ إِذَا وَقَبَ
۝٣ وَمِن شَرِّ ٱلنَّفَّٰثَٰتِ فِى ٱلْعُقَدِ ۝٤ وَمِن شَرِّ حَاسِدٍ إِذَا حَسَدَ ۝٥﴾

Say, "I seek refuge with the Lord of the daybreak (1) From the evil of what He created, (2) And from the evil of darkness when it settles, (3) And from the evil of those who blow in the knots, (4) And from the evil of the envier when he envies." (5)

Explanation

I seek refuge with Allāh ﷻ, the Creator of the morning light, from those things He created that have evil within them, and from the evil within the night when it spreads, and from the evil of those who practice witchcraft and those who are envious.

Lessons from Sūrah Falaq

1. Those who seek refuge with Allāh ﷻ, He will protect them from evil.
2. Witchcraft and envy are dangerous and harmful to the people.

سُورَةُ النَّاسِ